LIVING IN THE WILD: PRIMATES

MONKEYS

Claire Throp

Heinemann
LIBRARY

Chicago, Illinois

H **www.capstonepub.com**
Visit our website to find out more information about Heinemann-Raintree books.

To order:

☎ Phone 888-454-2279

💻 Visit www.capstonepub.com to browse our catalog and order online.

Edited by Abby Colich, Jilly Hunt, and Vaarunika Dharmapala
Designed by Victoria Allen
Picture research by Tracy Cummins
Original illustrations © Capstone Global Library Ltd 2012
Illustrations by Oxford Designers & Illustrators and HL Studios

Originated by Capstone Global Library Ltd
Printed and bound in China by CTPS

15 14 13 12 11
10 9 8 7 6 5 4 3 2 1

Library of Congress Cataloging-in-Publication Data
Throp, Claire.
  Monkeys / Claire Throp.—1st ed.
    p. cm.—(Living in the wild. Primates)
  Includes bibliographical references and index.
  ISBN 978-1-4329-5865-7 (hb)—ISBN 978-1-4329-5872-5 (pb) 1. Monkeys—Juvenile literature. I. Title.
  QL737.P9T47 2012
  599.8—dc22   2011012897

Acknowledgments
We would like to thank the following for permission to reproduce photographs: Corbis pp. 13 (© Keren Su), 16 (© Kevin Schafer), 17 (© Terry Whittaker/ Frank Lane Picture Agency), 26 (© Anup Shah), 32 (© Mary Ann McDonald), 35 (© John Stanmeyer/ VII); FLPA pp. 12 (Konrad Wothe/Imagebroker), 14 (Konrad Wothe/Imagebroker); istockphoto pp. 7 (© PeskyMonkey), 24 (© Chandra Widjaja), 39 (© Anna Chelnokova), 41 (© Brian Daly), 42 (© Nico Smit); National Geographic Stock pp. 36 (Frans Lanting), 38 (Medford Taylor); Photolibrary pp. 19 (Stéphanie Meng), 23 (Richard Packwood), 31 (Don Farrall), 44 (Robert Maier); Shutterstock p. 4 (© Uryadnikov Sergey), 9 (© Luis Louro), 10 (© Kjersti Joergensen), 15 (© jaana piira), 20 (© Eric Isselée), 21 (© markrhiggins), 22 (© Eric Gevaert), 25 (© tratong), 29 (© Sam Dcruz), 37 (© Katerina Lin), 40 (© Eric Gevaert).

Cover photograph of a macaque reproduced with permission of istockphoto (© Oystein Lund Andersen).

Every effort has been made to contact copyright holders of any material reproduced in this book. Any omissions will be rectified in subsequent printings if notice is given to the publisher.

Disclaimer
All the Internet addresses (URLs) given in this book were valid at the time of going to press. However, due to the dynamic nature of the Internet, some addresses may have changed, or sites may have changed or ceased to exist since publication. While the author and publisher regret any inconvenience this may cause readers, no responsibility for any such changes can be accepted by either the author or the publisher.

Contents

Some words are shown in bold, **like this**. You can find out what they mean by looking in the glossary.

What Are Primates?

What is that noise? It's deafening! Up in the trees above sits a howler monkey calling to let others know where the group is feeding. His call can be heard up to 3 miles (5 kilometers) away.

There are more than 350 **species** of primate, and these include monkeys—and humans! Our closest relatives are apes and monkeys. We are alike in many ways. Primates are **mammals**. This means they have hair or fur on their bodies and produce milk for their babies to drink.

This squirrel monkey is a primate. It is intelligent, likes to live in groups, and has eyes at the front of its head, just as humans do.

Common features

Primates have many things in common. They are mainly arboreal (live in trees). They are intelligent, which means they can think about problems and try to solve them. They can learn new skills and pass them on to infants. They also share a desire to be social (to live with others). Many species of primate live in large groups called troops.

Endangered

One thing nearly all primates have in common is that they are **endangered**. In many cases, the threats come from humans. **Habitat** destruction and hunting are just two of the problems faced by primates.

This map shows where in the world non-human primates live.

NORTH
AMERICA

EUROPE

ASIA

*Atlantic
Ocean*

AFRICA

*Pacific
Ocean*

*Pacific
Ocean*

SOUTH
AMERICA

*Indian
Ocean*

AUSTRALIA

Key

Non-human primate habitats

ANTARCTICA

What Are Monkeys?

There are over 250 **species** of monkey, which are divided into Old World monkeys and New World monkeys. About 30 million years ago, some Old World monkeys moved across the Atlantic Ocean from Africa to South America, perhaps on floating tree trunks or vegetation (plant life). Over a long period of time, the monkeys **evolved** and became what we today call New World monkeys.

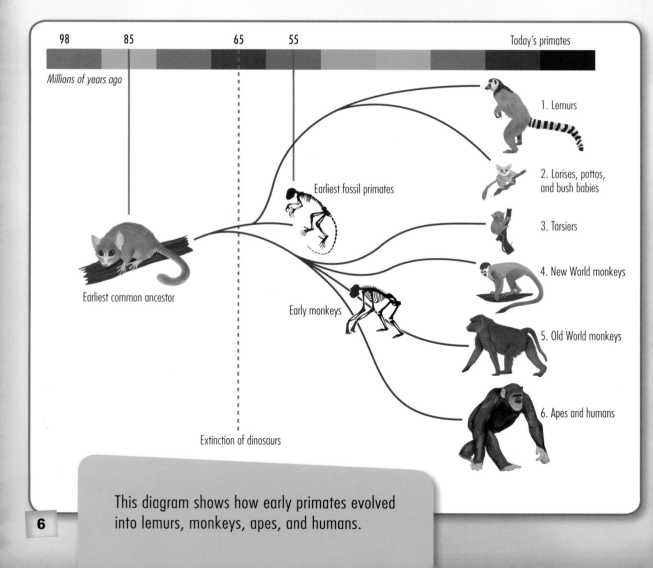

98   85   65   55   Today's primates

Millions of years ago

Earliest fossil primates

1. Lemurs

2. Lorises, pottos, and bush babies

3. Tarsiers

4. New World monkeys

Earliest common ancestor

Early monkeys

5. Old World monkeys

6. Apes and humans

Extinction of dinosaurs

This diagram shows how early primates evolved into lemurs, monkeys, apes, and humans.

Monkey features

One way of telling whether a monkey is Old World or New World is by its tail. New World monkeys tend to spend a lot of time in trees, so most of them have prehensile tails. Prehensile means "able to grasp." The monkeys can use their tails to hold onto branches as they move. Old World monkeys do not have prehensile tails. Some Old World monkeys live on the ground. They have bare sitting pads on their rear ends. New World monkeys do not have these pads.

Most monkeys have flat faces. Old World monkeys have large noses and forward- and downward-pointing nostrils. Most of them also have cheek pouches in which they can store food. New World monkeys have flatter noses with wider-set, sideways-facing nostrils.

Monkeys have hands that are very like humans' hands. They can grab, hold, and poke things. Old World monkeys have **opposable thumbs**, which make it easy for them to hold things.

This is a toque macaque, a type of Old World monkey.

How Are Monkeys Classified?

Classifying things is the way that humans try to make sense of the living world. Grouping living things together by the characteristics that they share allows us to identify them and understand why they live where they do and behave as they do.

Classification groups

The standard animal groups are kingdom, phylum, class, order, family, genus, and **species**. Sometimes, further classification involves adding more groups, such as a suborder or parvorder.

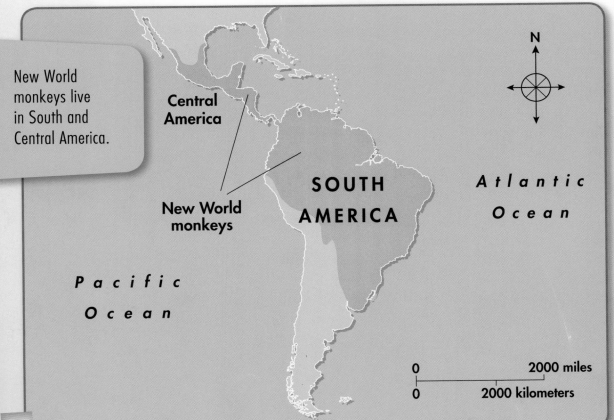

New World monkeys live in South and Central America.

Each of the standard groups contains fewer and fewer members. So, there are more animals in the class *Mammalia* (**mammals**) than in the genus *Saimiri* (squirrel monkeys). Animals are given an internationally recognized two-part Latin name. This helps to avoid confusion if animals are known by different common names in different countries. For example, the rhesus monkey has the Latin name *Macaca mulatta*.

New World monkeys

Haplorrhini (monkeys, apes, and tarsiers) is a suborder of primates. The suborder includes two parvorders: Platyrrhini (New World monkeys) and Catarrhini (Old World monkeys). Platyrrhini means "flat noses." Originally, New World monkeys were grouped into only two families. Recently, more families have been added. Not all scientists agree on the number of families. Some list four, while others list five.

The pyramid below shows how the bald uakari monkey is classified.

Kingdom: Animalia

Phylum: Chordata

Subphylum: Vertebrata

Class: Mammalia

Order: Primates

Suborder: Haplorrhini

Family: Pitheciidae

Subfamily: Pitheciinae

Genus: Cacajao

Species: Cacajao calvus

Old World monkeys

Old World monkeys and apes are sometimes known as *Catarrhines*, which means "drooping noses." There are two subfamilies: *Cercopithecinae* (baboons, macaques, guenons, mandrills, gelada, and vervets) and *Colobinae* (colobus monkeys, langurs, proboscis monkey, and snub-nosed monkeys). The first subfamily are omnivorous (they eat fruit, leaves, and small animals). They have cheek pouches and simple stomachs. The colobines are folivorous (they eat only leaves). They do not have cheek pouches, but they have complex stomachs.

Old World monkeys are actually a lot closer to apes and humans than to New World monkeys. This is shown by the number and organization of their teeth. They are also larger than New World monkeys and do not have prehensile tails.

The pyramid below shows how the proboscis monkey is classified.

Kingdom: Animalia

Phylum: Chordata

Subphylum: Vertebrata

Class: Mammalia

Order: Primates

Suborder: Haplorrhini

Family: Cercopithecidae

Subfamily: Colobinae

Genus: Nasalis

Species: Nasalis larvatus

10

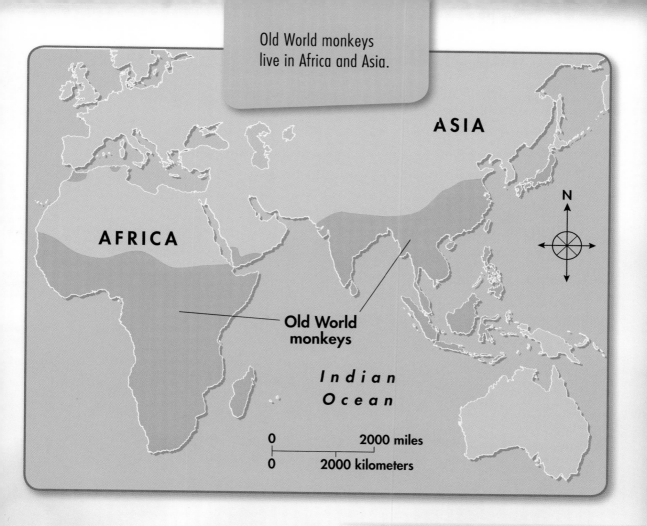

Old World monkeys live in Africa and Asia.

ASIA

AFRICA

Old World monkeys

Indian Ocean

| 0 | | 2000 miles |
| 0 | 2000 kilometers | |

Monkeys or apes?

Barbary macaques were once thought to be apes because they have only a stub of a tail, but they are in fact monkeys. They are still sometimes called Barbary apes. They are the only non-human primates to live in Europe. A group of Barbary macaques lives in Gibraltar, which is on the southernmost tip of Spain.

FRANS DE WAAL

Frans de Waal is a Dutch scientist. He has studied the behavior of primates, including how they bond together in groups. De Waal also studied macaques early in his career. He looked into how macaques get along with each other.

Where Do Monkeys Live?

A monkey's **habitat** has to provide everything the animal needs, from food and water to shelter. Monkeys live in a wide range of habitats.

New World monkeys

New World monkeys live in South and Central America. Many live in trees in **tropical rain forests**. It rains nearly every day in tropical rain forests, but it is also sunny and warm. Geoffroy's marmosets live in evergreen and semi-deciduous forests in Brazil. (Trees in semi-deciduous forests lose just some of their leaves in the colder seasons.) Black capuchins live in tropical or **subtropical** forests as well as mountain forests in Argentina.

This proboscis monkey lives in swampy forests and mangroves.

Old World monkeys

Old World monkeys live in Africa and Asia. Some are arboreal and live in tropical rain forests, such as the Diana monkey. Hamadryas baboons are found in sub-desert, plains, and savannahs. Savannahs are flat open spaces with little plant life. Trees are small and widely spaced. The baboons there have to make sure they stay close to watering holes. Geladas live on rocky cliffs in Ethiopia.

Macaques

Macaques can make their homes anywhere. Japanese macaques live in cold mountains and grow thick coats in winter. Crab-eating macaques live in hot, humid Asian forests close to water. They are good swimmers and are able to catch prey (animals hunted for food) underwater. This shows that **species** are able to adapt to different conditions over a long period of time.

Rolling snowballs is a good way for Japanese macaques to stay warm!

What Adaptations Help Monkeys Survive?

Different **species** of monkey have slightly different features that help them to live in their particular **habitat**. An **adaptation** is a feature that allows an animal to live in a particular place.

Habitat

Unlike many Old World monkeys, few New World monkeys are adapted for living on the ground. Only capuchins spend any amount of time on the ground when they **forage** for food. Most New World monkeys live in trees, so their prehensile tail is useful as a fifth limb. The tail has pads at the end that help it to grip branches or sometimes even bits of food. Spider monkeys do not have thumbs, which means their hands act as hooks to hold onto branches as they swing from branch to branch. Some Old World monkeys such as baboons have pads on their rear ends, because they spend more time sitting on the ground than jumping from tree to tree.

This spider monkey has a prehensile tail, which it uses to grasp branches.

ACHOO!

A species of snub-nosed monkey has been found in Myanmar (formerly called Burma). These animals sneeze when it rains! Local people have said that the monkeys can usually be found with their heads between their knees when it rains. This is to stop the rainwater from collecting in their upturned noses and making them sneeze. Unfortunately, like many other monkeys, the Burmese snub-nosed monkey is critically **endangered**.

Howler monkeys make extremely loud noises because it is difficult to see in the thick forest where they live. Sound carries a long way. Males have an extra large voice box with which to make noise.

Feeding

The saki has special teeth and a strong jaw that allow it to eat nuts that no other monkeys can eat. Leaf-eating monkeys have flat, grinding teeth, and their stomachs can break down the leaves and get rid of any poisons. Macaques and some other Old World monkeys have cheek pouches. If they see a predator, they can push the food into their pouches and escape somewhere safe to eat.

Eyesight

Monkeys rely on sight a lot more than smell. Their eyes are on the front of their heads, which allows them to judge distances easily. Being able to focus closely on things helps monkeys to find food. Howler monkeys eat leaves, and their color vision helps them to see which leaves are not poisonous.

The douroucouli, or night monkey, has a stronger sense of smell than most other monkeys. It also has bigger eyes, but it does not have very good color vision. These adaptations are all because the douroucouli is nocturnal. Color vision is not much use in the dark, but smell can help the monkey to find food when it cannot see clearly.

The douroucouli is the world's only true nocturnal monkey.

BRIGHTLY COLORED BABIES

Silvered langur monkeys (also known as silver leaf monkeys) give birth to bright orange babies, even though they are gray themselves. The baby will remain orange for about three months before its fur turns silvery-gray like its parents' fur. No one knows why this happens, but it might be so that the babies are easier to keep an eye on.

The pygmy marmoset has tiny hands but sharp claws. These features ensure that it does not fall off very thin branches when searching at the top of trees for insects.

17

What Do Monkeys Eat?

Animals eat other animals or plants and, in turn, they may be eaten by other animals. These links between animals and plants are called food chains. Many connected food chains add up to a food web. The more connections in a food web, the less affected it would be if one member of it died out.

In the diagram below, the number of monkeys is affected by the amount of fruit and leaves available for them to eat. If the forests are destroyed, less food will be available and the monkeys may die out. That will also affect animals like jaguars, since they eat monkeys.

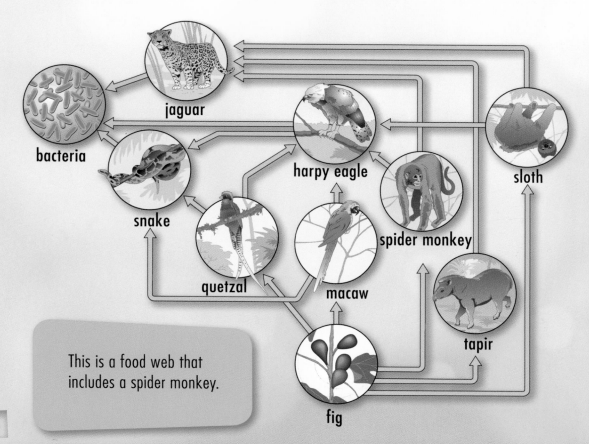

jaguar

bacteria

snake

harpy eagle

sloth

spider monkey

quetzal

macaw

tapir

This is a food web that includes a spider monkey.

fig

Producers and consumers

A food chain starts with a plant, because plants can make their own food. They are called producers. Animals are called consumers because they consume (eat) other animals or plants. Primary consumers eat plants, while secondary consumers eat other animals.

Animals that eat monkeys include **rain forest** eagles, snakes, crocodiles, and big cats such as ocelots and jaguars. These animals are carnivores (meat-eaters).

What do monkeys eat?

Monkeys are omnivores. This means that they eat fruit and leaves, but they also sometimes eat insects, small animals, or eggs. Macaques, like many other primates, also eat soil. There are several possible reasons for this. Soil rich in iron and kaolin (china clay) may help to soak up plant poisons. Soil may also contain certain **nutrients** that monkeys do not get from their normal food. Some soil is also able to kill off worms that live in the monkeys' stomachs.

This mona monkey is eating a fruit called papaya.

The life cycle of an animal covers its birth to its death, as well as all the different stages in between.

Mating

Different **species** of monkey behave differently when it comes to choosing a partner. Most Old World male monkeys have many partners. Female Barbary macaques mate with all the male members of the troop, so the father is never known for certain. Female geladas show that they are ready to mate when the skin on their rear ends and their chests becomes brighter in color.

The **dominant** male in a troop of mandrills has the brightest colors on its face. It also has a light purple rear end! This lets females know he is the best male to mate with. He fathers most of the young.

New World monkeys, such as uakaris, normally mate with only one partner. It is thought that the color of a uakari's face shows whether he has the disease malaria or not. Those who do not have it tend to have brighter red faces. These are the ones most females choose to mate with, because it means there will be less likelihood of their young catching malaria.

Pregnancy and birth

A monkey pregnancy usually lasts for four to seven months. Usually only one baby is born at a time in the wild, but some monkeys, including marmosets, may have twins. The black lion tamarin can have three or four babies at one time.

Crab-eating macaques usually give birth to only one baby, but sometimes they may have twins.

Young monkeys

Baby monkeys are born covered in fur and with their eyes open. They are helpless when first born and are sometimes carried in their mothers' mouths. They are soon able to cling onto their mothers' fur. A mother feeds the baby with her milk for several weeks. Mothers usually care for their young for a year to 18 months. Fathers care for babies in some species, such as marmosets, tamarins, and Barbary macaques. Females are usually unable to have more young until the baby is weaned (starts eating foods other than its mother's milk).

Babies are helpless when they are first born, but they are strong enough to cling onto their mother's fur.

Physical differences can be seen over the various life stages. Common marmoset infants do not have the white ear tufts that the older ones have, for example. The color of a number of species changes as they get older. Baboons are black with bright pink faces when first born, but they end up olive green or light brown, depending on the species.

The cycle begins again...

The age at which a monkey can reproduce (produce young) varies from species to species. Squirrel monkeys can give birth from the age of about two years, while the Hamadryas baboon has to wait for more than four years. Once monkeys are able to have their own babies, they start looking for a mate. Then the whole cycle begins again. Monkeys can live for about 20 years in the wild, but longer in captivity.

Playing and play fighting helps young monkeys such as these chacma baboons to learn new skills.

How Do Monkeys Behave?

Most monkeys live in large groups. Both visual and vocal communication is important to them.

Body language

Facial expressions are commonly used by monkeys. Staring is a threat, and baring teeth is a sign of aggression. Body position is also important. If a vervet monkey is on all fours with its tail coming over its head, it is feeling confident. Nose-to-nose greetings are used to suggest playtime or a grooming session.

Facial expressions help monkeys to maintain relationships with each other.

Vocal communication

Vervets have at least five different alarm calls. They let the other monkeys know which direction a threat is coming from. This ensures that the monkeys do not all climb trees if the predator is an eagle, for example. Many monkeys like to start the day with some calling and singing. This lets other monkeys know not to try feeding in their **territory**.

While most monkey communication is useful to others, monkeys have been known to lie. A researcher once saw a monkey work hard to dig up a plant to eat, only to have to abandon it when another monkey gave an alarm call. There was really no predator, however, and the other monkey raced over and stole the food!

Grooming

Grooming helps to get rid of ticks and fleas. It is also used to build and maintain friendships, show affection, and help make the social structure of a troop clear.

Geladas do not groom as much as other monkeys. Instead they chatter to each other all the time. Spider monkeys groom twice a day, but hugging is more important in their social relationships.

Macaques spend a lot of time grooming each other.

Social structure

Monkeys' social structures can be strict, and most troops are led by males. However, troops of squirrel monkeys sometimes have female leaders. Female geladas often run their social group, even though males are larger and stronger. The most common social group is one in which there are many males and many females. There is usually a **dominant** male monkey and a dominant female monkey. This means that there is less likelihood of violence within the group, because each monkey knows who is in charge.

The macaques' social structure means that high-ranked monkeys can take whatever they want from lower-ranked monkeys—even food from inside their mouths! Brown capuchins are led by dominant males, who get first pick of any food they find. Collared mangabeys live in troops of up to 35, with several males. They seem to live together peacefully, however.

Hanuman langurs spend about 80 percent of their life on the ground, moving on all fours.

Fighting

Males sometimes fight to compete for the right to mate with a female. They also fight to find out who is strongest and the best to lead a troop. Most monkeys prefer not to fight over territory and instead use vocal communication to warn other groups to stay away. This avoids energy-draining fights.

Infanticide

Many primates carry out infanticide when a new male takes over a troop. Infanticide is when the new male kills all the babies in the group. This behavior has been studied in groups of Hanuman langurs. It probably happens because while mothers are still feeding their babies, they cannot become pregnant. The new male wants to start fathering babies as soon as he can. The females stop making milk once their babies are dead, and so they can then mate and have more babies.

IT'S COLD!

Japanese macaques live in temperatures as low as -4 °F (-20 °C). One group has found hot springs heated by underground volcanoes to bathe in. However, only the highest-ranking females and infants and the dominant male are allowed in. The other monkeys have to shiver on the outside.

Caring for young

Females need to eat a lot to produce enough milk for feeding their babies. Marmosets often have twins, so other members of the family care for the babies while the mother searches for food. Arguments sometimes even break out over whose turn it is to groom the babies! Tamarins and langurs also have this system of child care.

Occasionally even a grandparent helps out! Scientists watching a group of Japanese macaques noticed a grandmother stepping in to watch and feed a baby when the mother was missing for a few days.

Feeding

Baboons are one of the few monkey **species** that can be predators. They can run extremely fast and kill large animals such as gazelles. They are also good swimmers and sometimes eat crabs. Allen's swamp monkeys have one of the more unusual methods of feeding. They lay grass and leaves on top of the water and then wait for fish to swim underneath. They then grab the fish for a tasty meal!

Capuchins let the rest of the group know if they find food by giving a series of loud whistles. If this attracts monkeys from another group, a fight breaks out. The winners get to eat the food. Angolan black-and-white colobus monkeys burp after eating. This is seen as a friendly action and is accepted by all the members of the group. Bacteria in leaf-eating monkeys' stomachs produce a lot of gas!

WATER FILTERING

Baboons in Saudi Arabia filter their drinking water so that it has fewer bugs and less dirt in it. They do this by digging holes next to ponds and waiting for the water to filter up through the sand before they drink it. The cleaner water helps them to stay healthy.

Local people think that black-and-white colobus monkeys are good weather forecasters. These monkeys become very quiet when bad weather is coming.

A DAY IN THE LIFE OF A MONKEY

Baboons are a type of monkey. They live in forests, grasslands, and scrublands in central and southern Africa. This is an example of a baboon's day.

TIME TO WAKE UP!

Although baboons spend most of their time on the ground, they usually sleep in trees. Baboons wake up early. Young baboons feed on their mothers' milk and then climb down to play. In the morning, baboons groom each other. This is important for their health, as they pick out ticks and fleas from each other's fur.

SEARCHING FOR FOOD

Eventually, small groups will join up to **forage** for food. They eat mainly grasses but also sometimes spiders and small animals. They are constantly on the lookout for lions, leopards, and other animals that might hunt them (predators). If one of these animals is spotted, a baboon will bark to warn the others.

It gets very hot in Africa in the middle of the day, so baboons rest in the shade until it is cooler. The baboons may try to find water, have a drink, and then spend some time grooming. Then they continue looking for food.

SHIRLEY STRUM

Shirley Strum is an expert on baboons. She has studied a group of olive baboons—known as the "Pumphouse Gang"—in Kenya since 1972. She has investigated the different roles of male and female baboons as well as ways in which people can help protect baboons and their **habitats**.

BED TIME!

In the evening, baboons often groom each other again. They split up into smaller groups to find a new place to sleep—either in a tree or on a cliff. They are safer from predators while on higher ground.

How Intelligent Are Monkeys?

Monkeys are less intelligent than apes, but more intelligent than other primates such as lemurs.

Living in groups

A large brain is the reason that monkeys are able to live in social groups. They have to know how to make friends and manage difficult relationships. Climbing the social ladder in the group is also something that males and females try to do. Grooming seems to be one way to make important friendships and make peace after fights.

Brown capuchins are very clever. This one is trying to break nuts by hitting them against each other on a rock.

Let's work together

Different **species** sometimes work together for protection against predators or to ensure they don't run out of food. While rivalries may sometimes exist between species, they are smart enough to know that sometimes it is better to have more eyes and ears available. Red colobus monkeys and vervets sometimes watch out for each other at water holes, for example.

Learning from parents

Young monkeys learn a lot from watching their parents. White-faced capuchins learn how to open clams by hitting the shells on branches or with rocks. They also discover how to rub their bodies with an anti-bacterial plant and the juices of other plants. This probably helps them to keep their fur free of fleas.

It has also been discovered that monkeys often pay more attention to females than males. In an experiment, vervet monkeys were better able to complete a task after seeing it demonstrated by a female than by a male. This may be because females tend to stay with the group in which they were born, while males move around. The females may be trusted more.

CLEAN YOUR TEETH!

In Thailand, long-tailed macaques have been seen flossing their teeth with pieces of hair. Adults may teach their young to keep their teeth clean, too. Mothers with infants have been seen flossing more slowly and for a longer time, exaggerating the action so that the infants can see more clearly what to do.

What Threats Do Monkeys Face?

It is thought that 50 percent of the world's primates are in danger of **extinction** in the near future. This is due to a number of reasons, all of which are linked to humans.

Habitat loss

The human population is expanding all the time. As more humans are born, more land is needed for food production and for housing. Humans are taking over the natural **habitats** of monkeys and other animals, too.

Deforestation is the cutting down of trees to clear land for farming or other non-forestry reasons. It is a major threat because so many monkeys live in trees. The Caqueta titi monkey is critically **endangered** due to deforestation in its Colombian home. The monkey was discovered 30 years ago, but conflict in the area meant that only very recently was anyone able to go there and confirm it as a new **species**.

The Caqueta titi monkey was put on the critically endangered list, since its habitat has been lost to farming. Only 250 of these monkeys are thought to exist. The monkeys are important because they help to spread seeds through their droppings, which in turn helps more trees to grow.

Black spider monkeys are not endangered at the moment, but they are very choosy about where they live. They will only live in primary forest, which is forest that has not been logged before or disturbed by humans in any other way. This means that the black spider monkey's status could change very quickly unless humans change their behavior.

The Amazon **rain forest** is being destroyed by the expansion of farms such as this one.

Climate change

Old World monkeys, in particular colobine monkeys, are likely to be hit hardest by global warming and climate change. The diet of colobine monkeys is based mainly on leaves, and the monkeys need to eat a lot of leaves to survive. If the temperature increases by just 3.6 °F (2 °C), more time will have to be spent resting because of the heat. The monkeys will therefore have less time to spend searching for food.

Hunting

"Bushmeat" is the term used for meat that comes from wild animals, including monkeys. In 2005 it was reported that seven million red colobus monkeys are taken for bushmeat each year. Many people often rely on bushmeat to survive. They need the money they get from selling it, and they eat it themselves in order to not go hungry. This makes it a difficult issue to deal with.

In rural areas of central Africa, about 80 percent of people's protein comes from bushmeat. This bushmeat hunter lives in the Democratic Republic of the Congo, in Africa.

Other human threats

The threats from humans do not stop with deforestation and hunting. Some monkeys are taken out of the wild and sold as pets or to perform tricks to make money for their owners. Others are killed because farmers consider them pests. Some monkeys face threats from several directions at once. For example, the Chinese golden monkey is caught for its meat, but also for its fur. With its habitat being destroyed, too, the monkey has little chance of survival unless major changes are made.

MONKEY TRADE FOR SCIENTIFIC RESEARCH

Monkeys have long been used for scientific experiments and medical research. About 70,000 non-human primates are used for research in the United States each year. There is a trade between countries in which primates are bred, such as China and Israel, and laboratories around the world. This trade means that animals can sometimes go on journeys of more than 40 hours in a cramped cage. Animal welfare groups are constantly trying to improve conditions for these primates.

Some monkeys are used to test medicines for diseases before they are tried on humans. They are kept in small cages and often live in pain from the diseases they have been given.

How Can People Help Monkeys?

Monkeys are close relatives of humans, and yet humans have brought them near **extinction**. We need to protect monkeys and other primates, and there are a number of ways to do this.

Conservation organizations

Wildlife organizations help monkeys not just by raising money, but also in practical ways. They can encourage local people to use solar cooking techniques, for example. Solar cooking relies on the sun for heat, so less wood is used. There is therefore less damage caused to the monkeys' **habitat**.

Conservation groups work to protect monkeys and their habitats. This man is feeding milk to a monkey that has lost its parents.

Eco-tourism

Eco-tourism can be used to help monkeys by providing an alternative source of income for local people. Many tourists are interested in seeing animals in the wild, but they often need a guide to show them where to go and how to behave with the animals. Local people can do this job and other jobs linked to tourism.

What can you do?

- You can join **conservation** groups, such as the World Wildlife Fund (WWF) and Conservation International, and perhaps donate some pocket money every now and then.

- Encourage your family not to buy furniture made from the wood of **rain forest** trees.

- If you go shopping for food with your parents, you can ask them to buy goods that have been produced in an environmentally friendly way. Food labels will give information on this. Fair Trade Certified goods ensure that money is earned by local people, which may mean they do not have to take part in activities that may harm monkeys.

- Finally, make sure you recycle as much as possible. This means that materials such as wood can be saved and reused, so that fewer trees will need to be cut down.

Read about monkeys and tell your friends and family what you find out. The more people who know about **endangered** monkeys, the better.

What Does the Future Hold for Monkeys?

Monkeys face many threats, and some **species** are likely to become **extinct** in the near future. At the moment, the species **extinction** rate across all animals is 1,000 to 10,000 times higher than it would be naturally (without humans).

On the positive side, however, many groups are working hard to protect monkeys and **conserve** their **habitats**. **Conservation** organizations like the WWF and **Endangered** Species International are working to show people throughout the world the danger some animals are in.

The golden lion tamarin's status has changed from critically endangered to endangered. There are still many threats to their safety, but their numbers have increased in recent years. This is partly due to reintroduction of captive-bred monkeys to wild populations.

Local people

Working with local people and encouraging them to feel pride in these wonderful animals is also essential to conservation. One conservation project in Ecuador encouraged local people to collect information on the critically endangered brown-headed spider monkey. The knowledge they gained helped them to fight an attempt by a mining company to buy land in the middle of the monkeys' habitat. They were able to show that the mining would have a negative effect on the monkeys. Noise and air pollution would also have affected the local human population.

Reintroduction to the wild

Recently, the idea of **reintroducing** zoo animals to the wild has become more popular and has been relatively successful. Zoos and sanctuaries create habitats that are very similar to the natural habitats of different monkeys. Animals from these zoos and parks have been successfully reintroduced to the wild.

It is important that we do not allow monkeys to die out. They deserve their place in the natural world. The more young people—like you!—who get involved, the better.

Barbary macaques live in troops of up to 40 monkeys.

41

Monkey Profiles

brown or black fur

long snout with nostrils on the end

tail (not prehensile) is carried in an arch shape

Species: Chacma baboon

Weight: Up to 88 pounds (40 kilograms)

Height [not including tail]: Up to 35½ inches (90 centimeters)

Length of tail: Up to 30 inches (75 centimeters)

Habitat: Desert, savannah, grasslands, **tropical** monsoon forests

Diet: Fruit, leaves, roots, insects, small birds, and **mammals**

Number of young: One infant born after 5 to 6 months of pregnancy. Females will give birth about every 18 months to 2 years.

Life expectancy: Up to 27 years

prehensile tail

bare, round black or brown face

reddish, light brown, or black fur

Species: Woolly monkey

Weight: 15 to 22 pounds (7 to 10 kilograms)

Height [not including tail]: 16 to 24 inches (40 to 60 centimeters)

Length of tail: Up to 31½ inches (80 centimeters)

Habitat: Rain forests

Diet: Fruits and leaves

Number of young: One infant born after 7 to 8 months of pregnancy. Females will give birth about once every 2 years.

Life expectancy: Up to 30 years

Glossary

adaptation body part or behavior of a living thing that helps it survive in a particular habitat

classify group living things together by their similarities and differences

conservation protection or restoration of wildlife and the natural environment

conserve protect from harm or destruction

dominant strongest; most powerful

eco-tourism form of tourism that allows people to observe wildlife and help protect nature

endangered living thing that is at risk of dying out

evolve change gradually over time

extinct living thing that has died out

extinction when a living thing has died out

forage look for food over a wide area

habitat natural environment of a living thing

mammal animal that has fur or hair, gives birth to live young, and feeds its young on milk from the mother

nutrient substance that provides a living thing with the nourishment it needs to grow and live

opposable thumb thumb that can face and touch the fingers on the same hand

rain forest forest with tall, thickly growing trees in an area with high rainfall

reintroduce put a living thing back into its natural environment

species group of similar living things that can mate with each other

subtropical regions of Earth that border the tropics

territory area of land that an animal claims as its own

tropical regions of Earth around the equator

46

Find Out More

Books

de la Bedoyere, Camilla. *100 Things You Should Know About Monkeys and Apes.* New York: Barnes and Noble, 2008.

Moore, Heidi. *Protecting Food Chains: Rain Forest Food Chains.* Chicago: Heinemann Library, 2011.

Solway, Andrew. *Classifying Living Things: Classifying Mammals.* Chicago: Heinemann Library, 2009.

Websites

http://animals.nationalgeographic.com/animals/photos/monkeys/
This website has lots of pictures of different species of monkeys.

www.sandiegozoo.org/animalbytes/t-monkey.html
Learn more about monkeys at this website.

Organizations to contact

World Wildlife Fund
www.wwf.org
WWF works to protect animals and nature, and it needs your help!
Take a look at its website to see what you can do.

Endangered Species International
www.endangeredspeciesinternational.org/index.php
This organization focuses on saving endangered animals around
the world.

Born Free USA Primate Sanctuary
www.bornfreeusa.org/sanctuary/
This organization provides a sanctuary for baboons, macaques,
and vervets, many of which come from abusive situations.

Index